101 REASONS NOT TO MURDER THE ENTIRE SAUDI ROYAL FAMILY

101 REASONS ^NOT^ TO MURDER THE ENTIRE SAUDI ROYAL FAMILY

Donald H. Carpenter

Cover design and interior drawings by

Charles Hooper

To order additional copies of this book, contact:
Xlibris Corporation
1-888-795-4274
www.Xlibris.com
Orders@Xlibris.com
18727

PREFACE

As the title indicates, in this book I discuss 101 reasons not to murder the entire Saudi Royal Family (Some who have a need for a humor enhancement might sarcastically insist that I actually discuss 101 opinions that are not good reasons for murdering the entire Saudi Royal Family!).

Most of the "reasons" originated from news stories that appeared (in various publications, such as the *New York Times* or *The Wall Street Journal*, or online) during 2001 and 2002, although variations on many of those stories had appeared much earlier.

The American public, and particularly the young people of America, probably cannot help but wonder what is behind our policy in the Middle East. It seems so contradictory, and so "NOT" in our national interest, at times, that anyone with an average intelligence who pays attention to the news must be somewhat puzzled by the actions of our government. Why do "THEY" hate us so? Are "THEY" our friends or our enemies? And why does that change so often?

We know that what the world needs is more peace and less war, so why do we not move in that direction? How many times, just since 1980, has the U.S. intervened somewhere militarily? Today, no one in the U.S., except for a few individuals generally regarded as "kooks" or "eccentrics", question the idea that the U.S. should be the world's policeman. How far we have come in just my lifetime.

Donald H. Carpenter
January 2003

1. They were at least partly responsible for the 9/11 World Trade Center attacks.

This has not been proven to date. It does appear that a good many of the hijackers involved, and possibly many more involved in the planning and financing of the terrorist attack, were from Saudi Arabia. And it is known that the Saudi Royal Family walks a *very* fine line in dealing with Islamic terrorists, religious fundamentalists, and the poor in their own country, while trying to hang onto power. Remember what happened to the Shah of Iran? Well . . .

However, it has simply not been proven at this point that the family was involved directly in the 9/11 attacks.

2. They finance terrorism all over the world in other ways.

Here the record is less clear. The combination of governmental expenditures, interlocking charities, and quasi-private businesses make it an interesting subject to explore. The problem would be how to prove it in an international court of law. Even then, the act of dispensing with the *entire* family would be mischievous at best, and perhaps unjustified murder at worst. I mean, what if they all weren't involved? We'll discuss that later. More work needs to be done here before this connection is most definitely established.

3.   They repress their own people.

This is definitely true. The people are very poor and repressed, in spite of the huge revenues generated by the oil reserves. But *hey*—they can always blame it on Israel, and they do. In no way is it the fault of the repressive policies of the government, which grants a virtual monopoly on lucrative goods and services to the Saudi Royal Family, its friends and cronies. The members of the Saudi Royal Family are all doing very well, obscenely well, due to the artificially granted privileges. Remember the prince who tried to give New York City $10,000,000 (that's $10 million!) after the 9/11 terrorist attack. His name is Prince Alwaleed bin Talal, and he's worth about $20 billion just by himself. Not bad for a nice Saudi boy.

But, unfortunately, if you murdered them for that reason, you'd have to murder the families of every Islamic-led government in the Middle East. Because they are all repressive by American standards. Or you would be inconsistent, and people would criticize you for that.

4.   They're rich.

Yes, they are—and how!!! But, and this may surprise some people, we still don't murder people just because they're rich. No one is seriously proposing murdering the Kennedys, or the Rockefellers, or Bill Gates (except maybe a Linux user or two), or Ted Turner (well, maybe some right wingers). In fact, with the Communists gone or seriously diminished, almost no society (maybe none) wants to eliminate its wealthy citizens anymore. They may criticize the rich in general, but that is about it. The disparity of wealth in the Middle Eastern countries, very much including Saudi Arabia, is about as great as in any region or country around the world. Now why is that simply not a surprise? Anyway, it's just not a good enough reason. Period.

5.   They're Arabs.

No, that won't cut it. We have a long, if somewhat creaky and inconsistent, history, in this country at least, of respecting differences in nationality. We have had shifting alliances with a whole host of different groups of peoples. The fact that a particular group is a certain nationality, tribe, etc. doesn't mean much to us. They can still be good people. Besides, we're talking about the Saudi Royal Family, not Arabs in particular. What is it about that particular group of people that commands, or demands, murder—if anything?

6. They haven't helped with the investigation into the 9/11 attacks.

There may be a point there, or at least they haven't helped enough. After all, they are caught between the masses in Saudi Arabia, and neighboring Islamic countries, and the enlightened world. If they help to investigate too publicly, they will incur the wrath of their own subjects. If you saw the profile of Prince Alwaleed bin Talal on *60 Minutes* a while back, you saw how he stood by while one of his subjects castigated Rudolph Giuliani for being a "lackey for the Jews", while the Prince's interviewer, Bob Simon, who is Jewish, was standing right there! No consideration. But it shows the mentality that the Saudi Royal Family is up against, and why they have to walk a fine line.

Someone suggested that they could move to America and get real jobs, but I don't think that is very likely to happen.

7. Bin Laden is a family member of a favored Saudi family.

Osama bin Laden is a member of a family very much favored by the Saudi Royal Family. The family gets multi-million dollar government contracts, and supposedly kicks back large sums to the Saudi Royal Family. Osama bin Laden supposedly is on the outs with the mainstream portion of his family, but his brothers stay in touch with him, and even his mother still visits with him (or she did up until 9/11)! Isn't that touching how his Mom stands by him? A mother's love never fails to delight! Even if your son is a world's record murderer-conspirator, he's still that lovable son you once held to your breast. Ahem.

However, we must remember that the Saudi Royal Family has supposedly officially denounced bin Laden, and he supposedly hates them very much. Sounds kinda suspicious to me, but that is the public story. There is not much, if any, evidence that the Saudi Royal Family had anything to do with planning any of bin Laden's activities. Maybe they financed some of them, but that still needs work. I wonder, though . . . if you favor the family of a mass murderer with lucrative government contracts, and then some of that family money makes it to the mass murderer, money being a fungible commodity, then doesn't that . . . ?

8. The Saudi Royal Family finances terrorism through charities, money laundering, etc.

This is entirely possible, although some would dispute that we have proven that. However, the Saudis do hate Israel, and the Jews, and they would do whatever they could to eliminate them. So it makes sense in a theoretical way that they would try to finance terrorism in an underhanded way. After all, the Arab states have to say that they support Israel's existence to the world, because they have never made the case for Israel's destruction; they simply want it to happen. They have been unable to make it happen militarily, but some cling to the strategy that they can make it happen through sheer terrorism, and they fund that terrorism in an underhanded way. However, it has simply not been proven that the Saudi Royal Family has been behind it. At least not yet.

9. They're Muslims.

Well, they say they are, and of course their remaining in power is contingent upon them continuing to convince the masses of Saudi Arabia that they are. But a growing number of clerics in Saudi Arabia itself, and in the Islamic world at large, seem to question that simple statement. If they are Muslims, some would say, then they seem to be very convenient ones. They probably act one way when in Saudi Arabia, or at least in public there, and an entirely different way when in private, or in another country, especially a non-Islamic country. But there are rumors of individual members watching risqué (by Islamic standards) television, reading scandalous literature, drinking alcohol, smoking (is that prohibited?), and visiting strip clubs (Gasp!)!

But, if you have the subjects of your country so deluded that they'll come by every week and kiss your shoulder or elbow, then you probably have them shielded from these horrors. It is a fine line to walk, fooling the citizenry completely and keeping them in poverty, when at any moment they could wake up and a mass revolt could be triggered. It could happen tomorrow . . .

Anyway, we don't kill people because of their religious beliefs. We just don't, that's all.

10. They wear funny clothing.

Well, we can dispose of this one easily enough. Many people in different parts of the world—even in different parts of this country—do things that are different, or wear clothing that is different. That is part of the diversity of life, that different people do different things. It is true not even just among groups, but within seemingly homogeneous groups as well. It is part of the general idea of tolerance that we peacefully respect and allow for that, without trying to stamp out all differences. Just think if someone held it against you for wearing long hair, or cutoff jeans, or a halter-top, or a baseball cap. And yet to the Saudis, all of that might seem funny as well.

Also, killing someone for wearing funny clothing might be considered an extreme reaction. I think in most countries it may even be against the law. I remember being in the Memphis airport and seeing a man wearing a Russian fur hat (Yes, it *was* mid-winter at the time.). A friend traveling with me said that the man was provoking violence by wearing such a ridiculous hat in public. But even my friend didn't actually initiate any violence, and the man passed by without any harm.

11. They're religious fanatics.

Actually, they're not. They're fun-loving rich people who like to hunt animals, go shopping in Western stores, watch American TV, eat many foods, including pork, drink many fluids, including alcohol, have sex in semi-wild positions, and so forth. This doesn't mean that every single one of them does these things, but some of them do. They are actually treading a very fine and dangerous line in their own country by monopolizing and/or controlling all the wealth, but tolerating the extremist viewpoints from others that members of the Saudi Royal Family do not hold themselves.

Rich people, especially the children of the rich, like to experiment with different stuff. They may dabble in Marxism, or even fascism, go to a monastery, live the high and fast life, or do other things that seem extreme in the light of their surface religious background or family upbringing. They may switch lifestyles in a moment's notice, so to speak, just to kill boredom, since many often have no full-time, permanent jobs to occupy their time. So this is not that unusual. But the Saudi Royal Family placates the religious extremists in its own country; the members of the Saudi Royal Family are not themselves in that category. But shhhh—don't tell anybody from that neck of the woods.

12. They hate Christians.

Well, maybe—but then again, maybe not. They probably don't look on most Christians as a threat, except maybe for some of the more radical sects that populate the Middle East. In the Middle East, religious intolerance runs very high, and the Saudi Royal Family is in the thick of all that mess. However, they're simply not very religious themselves for the most part, except in a "higher", secular way, and so they don't take personal offense at someone for simply being a Christian, especially of the American variety. They probably simply don't care, except . . .

Again, they are walking that very thin line between holding on to their power and control and wealth, and losing it to the religious fanatics within their own country. So if the *vox populi* says hate the Christians, they'll hate the Christians. If it says hate them every other Thursday and have a public parade at the same time, they'll do that. In a way, they are the puppets of their own puppets.

13. They hate Jews.

I think this one is pretty definite. It is everywhere in their actions, and in the actions of almost everyone in that part of the world, certainly those in the Islamic community. The attitude predates the establishment of the state of Israel, and it permeates every level of Arab and Islamic society. Those of us in the United States (unless we are Jewish) really have no idea how deep and strong the feeling really is. It is almost like an instinct, it is so deeply ingrained. It makes one wonder how it will ever be expunged from the souls of peoples.

The Saudi Royal Family is certainly not immune to this. And even if they felt differently, they would still pretend to believe it in order to cling to power. They simply have too much to lose. Their true feelings might be hard to gauge, if they ever stopped long enough to have independent thoughts about the matter. But they cannot allow themselves the luxury of contradicting the popular sentiment of the masses under them even for one second, not on this crucial issue. They'd be better off drinking a case of Wild Irish Rose every Saturday night in the center of downtown Jeddah than to fail to hate the Jews.

However, having said all that, I doubt if many people, even Jewish people outside of some areas of Israel, would say that that means we can kill 'em all and let Allah sort 'em out!

14. They hate women.

Well, here you might have to break it down into individual members of the family. Certainly, the female members don't hate women, at least not in a general sense. But at the same time, it is the men who rule the roost in this family. And they are certainly against the independence of women in any meaningful way. Once again, though, we run into this fundamentalism that they have to cater to in order to hang onto their money and power. It is a factor that influences their behavior in countless ways. And no doubt the women members of the family have become just as corrupted over time as the men in this regard. They will sacrifice what they know is morally right in order to cling to what they have. The money and the power they have bring them many things, and they will wear the veils, and sacrifice careers, and so forth, and also make those decisions for countless thousands (or millions) of others, in order to keep that money and power.

15. They don't allow freedom of the press.

Well, they really can't. The public wouldn't like it very much, and it would cause great unrest. The Saudi Royal Family, by catering to the masses in their country, has built up a sort of popularity, fragile though it is. So they are popular in a way that, for instance, the Shah of Iran and his regime weren't, at least not at the time of the Islamic Revolution. The masses in Saudi Arabia are not very open to freedom of speech of the type that we have here in America. They probably would not be very open to allowing any sentiments that opposed their religious tenets, or even to allowing for open criticism of the Saudi Royal Family. It's funny how it works in both directions with an authoritarian ruler, or set of rulers, especially if they cloak themselves in royalty. As long as they make an effort to keep the majority happy, then the majority will brook no criticism of those rulers, even if many individual members of the masses have many individual disagreements with the government. The abstention from criticism of the rulers becomes a tradition in itself, and the longer it lasts, the more difficult it becomes to throw it off. Honest differences of opinion on political and religious issues are still a long way off, and flag burning and porn are even further off, at least for the general public.

However, many governments around the world are not as advanced as the United States in allowing that level of freedom of speech, and you can't kill people for giving the public in the country they rule what that public wants.

16. They don't allow freedom of religion.

True, and this falls into the same category already mentioned: the public, and the clerics who set the tone of belief in Saudi Arabia, wouldn't stand for it. To allow someone to openly believe in something besides what the public and the clerics believe is too much of a stretch at this point. If you don't believe me, go there and preach something—anything—besides Islam. And if you preach anything, to be on the safe side, it had better be fundamentalist Islam. None of this Reform Islam, or any other kind of watered-down version, thank you very much.

Again, though, how much of this do the members of the Saudi Royal Family really believe, especially when they leave Saudi Arabia and travel to other parts of the world? After all, they vacation (some even live) in fancy places, drink alcohol, refuse to wear the traditional clothing, engage in high finance—all kinds of things that they would never do, at least not in public, while in Saudi Arabia.

None of the Islamic countries, certainly not the ones in the Middle East, allow for diverse views where religion is concerned. The more insecure proponents of a view, religious or otherwise, are, the less tolerant they are, because they suspect very deeply that others will change their preference if given that freedom.

17. They hate Israel.

Well, duhhhh. In spite of some commentators (Thomas Friedman, David Halberstam, Bernard Lewis) trying to deny it for some reason, it's pretty clear that the main reason THEY (portions of the Middle Eastern Muslims) hate the U.S., and its people, is because the U.S. supports Israel financially, and on key votes in the United Nations. All you have to do is ask any of the leaders who acknowledge that they, and their underlying supporters, hate the U.S., and they will tell you that it is because of our support of Israel. If we don't recognize that, then we are fooling ourselves. If it were merely loose Western values, they would hate the European community that much more, because they are way more liberal than we are. Check out their TV versus ours, or their nude beaches. Those merely draw many fundamentalists rather than repel them.

Now does the Saudi Royal Family really hate Israel? I think so, even though they must have more of a love-hate relationship with it. After all, if Israel didn't exist, the Saudi Royal family would not have that unifying element to hold their country together, with them at the top. Creating an enemy that all the people hate, especially an external enemy, in order to bind the people together underneath you—that is one of the oldest ploys of the dictator. It still works well today, especially when you control the media, like the Saudi Royal Family does.

18. They aren't sincere in their efforts to fight terrorism.

This is true, but again you have to look at their ultimate motivation, which is simply to remain in power and enjoy their riches. Those riches have been generated, not through free market capitalism (what riches of that level ever are?), but through "businesses" protected from competition, and through kickbacks from those "businesses" owned by others who want to do business with the government of Saudi Arabia, or to otherwise conduct business in that country.

If they don't really fight terrorism, it is because they perceive that the people under their rule don't really want them to. The prevailing sentiment among the powerful clerics in their country is definitely in support of terrorist efforts against Israel, and against the U.S., because we support Israel. If ever we needed evidence of that, it was bin Laden's own statements on his videotape of December 2001, or in the statements of numerous terrorist leaders. It is as plain as daylight. Trust me on this one: they don't mind the liberal sexuality of Europe or Brazil at all (in fact, when they're out of the country, they probably enjoy it all), or gambling, or even abortion (When was the last time you heard of a Muslim-American rally against abortion? They don't happen.), but they do mind American support of Israel. And they mind it very much.

Remember that dictators, just like democratically elected leaders, must maintain popular support among the masses if they want to remain in power for any length of time. The situation is no different in Saudi Arabia.

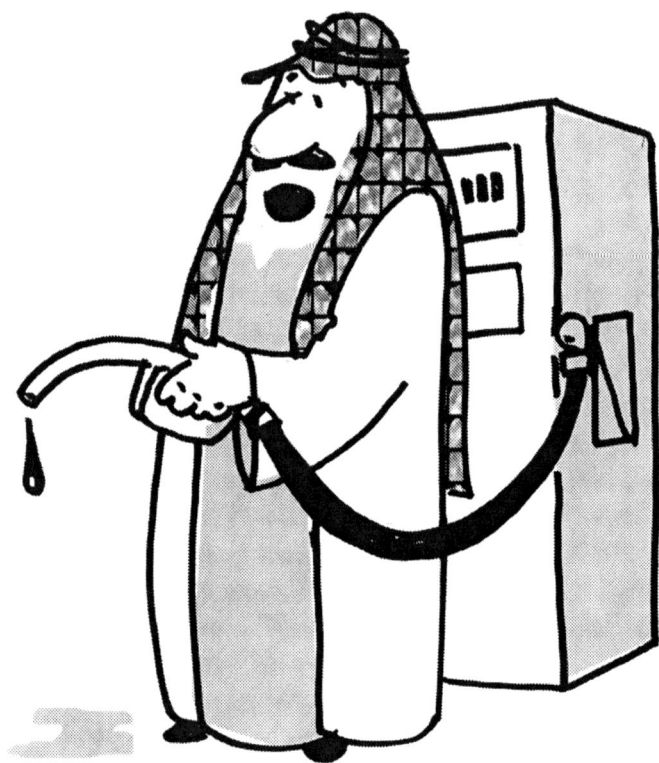

19. They control the world's oil supply.

Not all of it, but certainly the biggest chunk. But so what? They can't drink it, although some of their actions make you think that they think they can (or even that they already have). They have to sell it at the best price they can get, in the greatest quantity. In other words, they must sell at the optimum price. Too low of a price, and they won't make the most profit. Too high of a price, and they won't sell as much (and therefore still won't make as much profit), at least over a period of time.

Remember that, in 1979, the oil-producing countries (or certain of their actions) actually caused the price of gasoline to soar very high (as high as $1.30/gallon by 1981 in Louisiana, where I lived at the time—and Louisiana was one of the least expensive states for gasoline). By 1986, the price had dropped to lows of around $0.65/gallon, and now, 20 years later, the price is not really as high as 1981 levels. This is particularly true if you consider that the amount of federal and state taxes per gallon has increased dramatically during that 20-year period, and if you further consider the effects of inflation during that period.

So the Saudis may have physical control of much of the world's oil supply, but don't overestimate their power to set prices for any great length of time. Otherwise, they would have jacked it up and kept it up, and said "*Fuck you*" to any American objections. Because, believe me, that is the way they feel towards us. But they simply can't do it.

FOR SALE

20. They take their oil millions (or billions) and try to "buy up America."

This is an old accusation that started back around 1973, at the time of the first Arab oil embargo, when OPEC first flexed its muscles. In the years that followed, a lot of news reports inflamed the public, who feared that the Arabs who were getting rich off of the oil revenues were using those profits to buy assets in America. The U.S. stock market was down during most of the 1970s, and recessionary conditions kept hitting, so there were bargains for rich foreign investors.

It's an old story, one that replayed itself in the 1980s with the Japanese, before their economy tanked in the 1990s. Sometimes, economic conditions in a country become better than they ever have been, usually because of some anomalous conditions that have never occurred before. For the rulers and powerful families (are they ever not the same?) of such a country, the flood of riches causes them to look at relatively cheap investments in foreign countries, including the U.S. There were probably several less-threatening equivalents to what the Arabs and the Japanese did with other countries (maybe Great Britain or Germany) in years past. Usually, those types of surges in international investments end after a few years at most, and sometimes substantially reverse themselves when conditions in the purchasing country turn sour. Don't worry about this one.

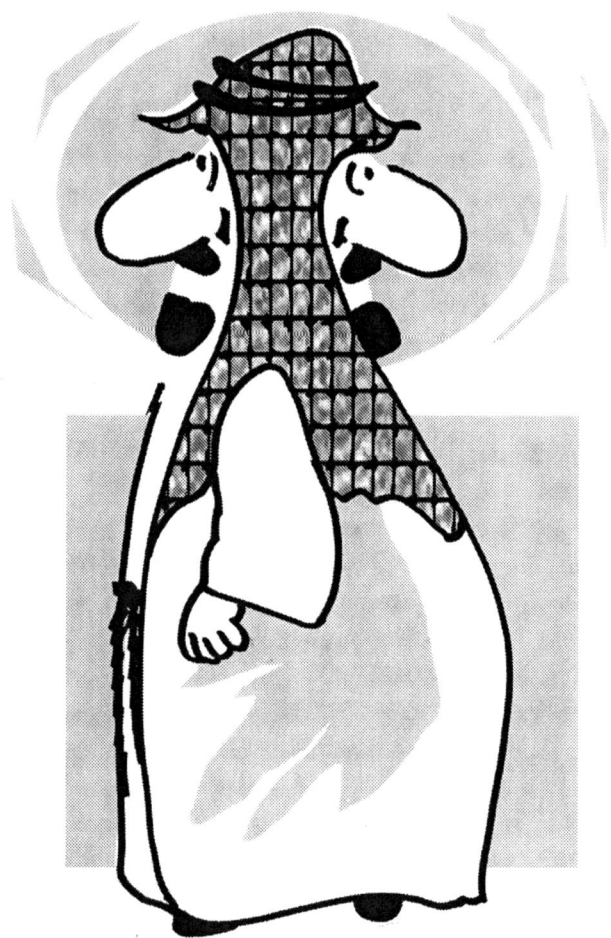

21. They're hypocrites.

Well, they definitely are, in the sense that they do one thing at home and another abroad, both in politics and in their personal lives. Many of us do just that, but we don't run a country. In some ways, one could get the idea that the Saudi Royal Family really wants to move its country forward into the 21st century. For example, very quietly, many women are operating businesses and going to college in Saudi Arabia. If the masses woke up to that, there could be a revolution. On the other hand, Saudi Arabia was one of only two countries to recognize the Taliban government in Afghanistan as of September 11, 2001, breaking off recognition only after the mass murders. And of course the Taliban was probably known more for its mistreatment and suppression of women than for anything else, possibly even its harboring of Osama bin Laden.

I've already mentioned how members of the Saudi Royal Family act differently, almost in the hedonistic manner we expect of the superrich, and also how they are desperate to retain power in their country, and therefore hang onto the wealth resulting from that power. So they run into a situation common to powerful rich people, particularly those who don't make it in the truly free market, offering goods and services the public wants and needs at competitive quality and price, but rather depend on a quasi-monopoly of sorts, backed by governmental power and privilege. They must cater to things the masses want other than quality goods and services, since due to the monopoly those factors don't play as much of a part as they would in a free market.

22. They claim diplomatic immunity when they aren't even entitled to it.

I don't know why this one just flat pisses most people off so much, but it does. I think there's something about a foreigner being allowed to get away with a crime (sometimes even murder) in the United States by claiming diplomatic immunity. There is a good reason for diplomatic immunity (to protect diplomatic personnel from being persecuted because of political differences between two countries), at least on the surface, but in fact it probably has outlived its usefulness. If a country were mad enough at another country, they would just ignore it, or claim the personnel were really spies. Pancho Villa just flat ignored it back around 1915, and allowed his troops to invade the British embassy and arrest one of its diplomatic employees. And of course, the U.S. waived diplomatic immunity in the Tyler Kent case in 1940. But it does still exist, and it still pisses many people off.

But when a member of the spoiled Saudi Royal Family claims the immunity even when she is not entitled to it, then that is certainly grounds for an even higher than normal level of pissoffola. In December 2001, Princess Buniah al-Saud, a niece of King Fahd (he's the Big Dude), claimed diplomatic immunity while under investigation for various alleged crimes in the Orlando, Florida area. Then, after the sheriff's office accepted her claim of diplomatic immunity (anybody want to lay down any money that she did or didn't have Uncle King's permission to do so?), she went to stay at a $525 per night suite in an Orlando hotel. The investigators caught up with her there, after learning that she was not entitled to diplomatic immunity.

Ahhh, the children of the superrich—what will we do with them?

23. They actually have their Muslim clerics on the government payroll.

Yes, this one is true as well. The clerics are employed by the government, so you have a situation of dueling tensions. The Saudi Royal Family is under pressure from the clerics to run a more fundamentalist state, but the clerics are under pressure because the government pays their salaries. And they don't dare quit, at least most of them don't, because it is difficult for fundamentalist religious leaders to do much except spout religious talk. And if they ever think that someone suspects the game might be up, they start to get a little nervous ("What do you mean 'work for a living?'").

So they don't pretend to have anything but an official state religion. And to think we blamed the Commies all those years for restricting freedom, and blindly ignored the fundamentalist countries. We used to criticize the Commies for taking young people at birth and indoctrinating them into a system before they could think for themselves ("brainwashing" them was how we termed it). Now let's see—who else do we know who does that same thing???

24. They even discriminate against other Muslims who are minorities.

This is how strict the society in Saudi Arabia is: they even discriminate against other Muslims, such as Shiite Muslims (most Saudis are Sunni Muslims). Even for small differences in beliefs that Muslims in other countries might consider trivial, the Saudis persecute them through the organization known as the General Presidency of Promotion of Virtue and the Prevention of Vices, which enforces Saudi Arabia's harsh version of Islam. They arrest the Shiites at will, raid their mosques, sentence them to physical beatings and jail sentences for defending themselves against physical violence from other Muslims, and then double the punishment when they try to appeal their sentences. Would the Shiites do any differently to the Sunnis if they had the opportunity? Does it matter?

It should be clear by now that Saudi Arabia is one of the most repressive countries in the world, by any standards, clearly as much so as many notorious left-wing and right-wing dictatorships throughout history, such as the USSR, Paraguay, South Africa, Italy under Mussolini, the People's Republic of China, Cuba, and Nicaragua under Samoza. If they persecute other Muslims, think what they would do with Christians, Jews, agnostics, atheists, Buddhists, Sikhs, etc. It is true that sometimes people persecute those who are closest to them, especially if the numbers of the close minority are threatening. However, in Saudi Arabia's case, no other minorities are even allowed the chance to get larger; they are, for all practical purposes, forbidden.

25. They destroy monuments and buildings that belong to "unapproved" groups.

This one really shows the infantile nature of their minds. It is fairly well known how, prior to September 11, the Taliban in Afghanistan destroyed some carvings of Buddha in the walls of some mountains. When they couldn't accomplish it any other way, they "dynamited" the walls until the carvings were destroyed. The world reacted in horror; at least, those who read about it did.

But the Saudis are just as bad! One day we'll wake up to the fact that the Taliban had only to look to the Saudis as an example! As of January 2002, the Saudis were destroying an 18th century castle from the Ottoman Empire that was located in the city of Mecca. It was and is part of an ongoing strategy to destroy monuments from earlier eras and religions to keep people from traveling to them and venerating them as shrines. The castle is to be replaced with residential buildings and a hotel. The building of that new project was awarded to the bin Laden group (who else??).

Are the Saudis just destined to be the most intolerant people of all time, or at least in modern times, with their close-minded views enforced by the Saudi Royal Family? Have they forgotten the power of TV? Do they think they won't have *Sex and the City* (or something similar) in a few years?

It's enough to make some anti-fanatics want to slip some pork in their food, or maybe an oyster or a scallop. Doncha just hate intolerant people??

26. They eat their young.

This one we can definitely put to rest. No one has come forward with any credible evidence that they do any such thing, nor have any individuals within the group ever advocated doing that.

27. They won't let non-Muslims visit Mecca or Medina.

This is true, and the reason generally given is just that they are important shrines for Islam, and that it would be inappropriate to let non-Muslims visit. Of course, they did let Spike Lee film part of *Malcolm X* at Mecca—or did they? Well, it doesn't matter. Not everything can be open for everyone in the whole world to see. Mormons don't allow non-Mormons (are those Gentiles, too?) in their temples. What would religions be without a little discrimination, or even intolerance? And remember that Islam is a state religion in Saudi Arabia, and the top officials all adhere to it (Did I manage to say that with a straight face?). And by the way, why would someone want to visit a shrine of a religion they don't believe in? Curiosity, of course—a trait much disapproved of in Saudi Arabia.

28. They're in bed with Big Business.

You can bet the farm on this one. They are in up to their scalps with Big Business interests from all over the world, primarily those concerned with Big Oil. Did you ever wonder what would happen to those countries, and the rulers who rule them, if they didn't have some kind of natural mineral wealth? They would actually have to develop products instead of just relying on location. They would have to use their minds instead of just letting others come to them. What if we developed an oil substitute tomorrow, or cut our use by two-thirds? The process has actually already started to happen. Remember what happened to Mexico in the 1980s? Louisiana?? It could happen in an even more dramatic way to Saudi Arabia.

Do you think that maybe the Saudi Royal Family has already mapped out their escape route? Kind of like Batista did? Diaz? Duvalier? Samoza? Fujimori? You can bet on that one, too!

29. They want American troops to leave the country.

Here is an interesting example of how the Saudi Royal Family walks a fine line. The U.S. sent troops in at the time of the Persian Gulf War. Depending on whom you believe, there was a threat to Saudi Arabia from Iraq. Supposedly Iraq was going to attack Saudi Arabia, just like it did Kuwait. That issue has never really been publicly debated, but for whatever reason, the Saudi Royal Family let us station troops there. It is a perfect example of how there is much animosity between Arab states, and how Israel and the Good Ole USA are convenient whipping boys in between inter-Arab wars. When Iraq supposedly threatened Saudi Arabia, there was almost unanimity among Arab governments to resist them (What a disaster it would be to have Iraq conquer all the other Arab dictatorships in the area!). So the Saudi Royal Family let the troops in.

But the crazies—the religious fanatics—never liked having U.S. troops in the country. Osama bin Laden used the presence as one of his main issues in creating a wave of terror against the U.S. So the Saudi Royal Family is now giving in to that demand (to remove the troops) to placate the crazies, after getting them to accept the presence under the supposed threat of an Iraqi invasion.

30. They let American troops in the country.

For a change of pace, this is a reason to murder them all from the point of view of their own fanatical countrymen, and their fellow travelers in other religious circles. The argument goes like this: they should never have allowed troops from the Satanic United States to be stationed in such a holy country (Do you ever wonder if the fanatical Islamic charge that the U.S. is under Satan's control could result in the largest conversion of people to Devil worship that has ever occurred in history—as a backlash to the charge—kind of like listening to rock n' roll after your parents told you not to?? Just a thought . . .).

Anyway, many of those who never wanted the troops there in the first place, and want them removed now, are among the most virulent enemies of the Saudi Royal Family. It is another example of the fine line the Saudi Royal Family walks in order to hold on to power and to their riches (How long can this possibly last?). It is also another example of the way that government is used by the wealthy to perpetuate not only their wealth, but also the great disparity of wealth that is so often criticized by social activists.

As for taking the troops out, it may not be such a bad idea. Let the Saudis defend themselves against their Arab enemies (They don't have to worry about their supposed #1 enemy—Israel—attacking them.). By the way, did you ever notice how the Saudis foment the hatred of Israel, but don't seem to get involved too directly in the military campaigns against Israel? Well, whether you noticed it or not, the religious crazies (and the people who finance them behind the scenes) have begun to notice it—quite clearly!

31. They try to pretend that they are America's friends when they are really not.

The Saudi Royal Family plays an elaborate game, as we have already discussed, with trying to live a modern, Western-style life when they can (and who can blame them there?), and with mollifying the fundamentalists at home. They also play an elaborate game with trying to convince the U.S. and its citizens that they are our friend and ally, while at the same time looking the other way for terrorists, and actively pursuing their hatred of Israel.

The two strands actually are bound together like a rope. In order to lead the good life, they must pacify the religious nuts, and part of that is hating the great "Satan" America ("Hail America!"), at least in public. The real fact is that they rather like America, at least its own rich citizens, and they like to hobnob with the beautiful people everywhere. The religious nuts in their own country know that, but they look the other way on the Saudi Royal Family's antics because they are more interested in hating those they want to hate. It's all a game, man!

32. They don't really believe in religion or Islam.

I think it's fair to say that they don't take it all literally, as many people in most societies don't. When the major religions were created, possibly as an attempt to explain what the world was all about (or possibly to control other people!), the founders laid down so many rules, and tried to include so many things that are hard to believe with the benefit of modern-day knowledge. Therefore, it is hard for many people nowadays to accept it all at face value. While they may not be able to disprove it, they note that all that happened many years ago, and the fact that it hasn't happened in modern times, when various events could be more definitely verified, raises their suspicions that it might be mostly myth.

And people want to have fun, without being bound by a bunch of religious rules. They want to cut up, gamble, have sex, drink beer, cuss a little here and there, and even cheat their neighbor, if they can get by with it without causing too much of a problem.

However, fundamentalist religion has a strong appeal to those who have no goals in life, who can't see much in the future, and who are looking for a cause. Therefore, it fits in perfectly with many in Arab countries, where the wealth is controlled by a few, and freedom is suppressed: there is no free speech or economic freedom. What they really need is a taste of freedom (even sinful activity! Shhh!!) and a chance at economic opportunity. That would knock the religious fundamentalism out of their souls. A little sinful activity goes a long way ☺.

33. They claim to have a democracy when they don't.

Well, wouldn't you, if you had a repressive dictatorship and wanted to pretend otherwise? There may be some "show" elections of sorts, but don't ever mistake Saudi Arabia for a real democracy. However, even dictators must have popular support if they are going to survive for long. And the Saudi Royal Family does have popular support, in a sense. As long as they placate the clerics (By the way, how did they get to be clerics? Can I be one, too? There are a few people I'd like to pass a death sentence on!), then their chances of remaining in power are greater. And, as we have seen, the clerics will overlook a little sinnin' here and there if they can get a little power themselves.

You see, as with all fanatical religions, very few people really accept it all the way and follow the radical teachings to the max. However, it only takes a relatively small number to create a lot of misery in the world. Even the clerics don't really believe all that they preach. They want to retain their own power, and to do that, they need followers. To get followers, you need to cater to that hard core, because they are the ones who believe most forcefully in their radical viewpoint. To put it another way, the true believers believe more so than the moderates about the things they believe in. Therefore, it takes less of them to form a powerful nucleus, and the rulers pay more attention to them, because they set the tone of the debate.

But if Saudi Arabia is a democracy, then Idi Amin is a vegetarian.

34. They drag their feet on investigating funding of terrorism in their country.

Well, why wouldn't they? After all, they supported the Taliban, or at least they were one of only two countries to recognize the Taliban government. And most of the 9/11 terrorists were Saudi citizens. Osama bin Laden is a former Saudi citizen with many important family members still in important positions in Saudi Arabia. Why on earth would the Saudi Royal Family want to stop supporting terrorism, and suddenly start investigating it???

They drag their feet on U.S. requests to investigate Saudi Arabian charities and businessmen who might be supporting terrorism, claiming that the U.S. government has not provided enough evidence to freeze bank accounts. Are we to understand that the Saudi Royal Family is now angling for the title of "Civil Libertarian Family of the Year"? If so, this would be big news, especially in a country that harshly hands down capital punishment and cuts off hands. This is the same country where no freedom of religion is tolerated, no free speech is tolerated, no freedom of association is tolerated, etc., etc. Yet now they want evidence!

35. They continually go through the motions of trying to change their ways.

Recently, it made the news that the Saudis were trying to change some of their antiquated habits. Crown Prince Abdullah bin Abdul Aziz al-Saud (did you catch the *bin* in his name?), the 77-years-old ruler of Saudi Arabia, is leading the way. He cut import taxes from 12% to 5% (Wow!), tried to stimulate the economy, which is burdened by 25% unemployment (How'd it get so bad in the first place? Maybe he should have cut that first!), criticized large kickbacks the Saudi Royal Family gets on government contracts and other business deals (Say, why doesn't he just stop that dead in its tracks?), and proposed that government contracts be awarded to the best person or company rather than because of connections to the Saudi Royal Family (Again, why not simply stop the practice instead of just suggesting it?).

Now get this: he still criticizes Israel, and U.S. support of Israel! You know, it's funny how familiar that sounds! Some folks never change: I've heard of knee-jerk liberals before, but how about knee-jerk Nazism? :::::Sigh:::::

In spite of its oil wealth, Saudi Arabia is an economic quagmire, with little or no hope for its youth, unless they are born to the Saudi Royal Family or its friends. It's always that way in a country that penalizes competition and relies instead on cronyism in any form. High unemployment, low wages, low growth, repressive policies—you would think that having a semi-monopoly on such a needed natural resource as oil would cause a country to be prosperous, but it ain't that simple, Charlie.

But at least the Prince did finally acknowledge that most of the 9/11 hijackers were Saudi Arabian nationals. Way to go, fella!

36. They pretend to monitor bank accounts that might be used to support terrorists.

The Saudi Royal Family, in its role as ruler of the government, often pretends to monitor bank accounts, usually at the request of the U.S. government, and especially since 9/11. They first go through a show of pretending to resist the U.S. request, then they quietly (but always leaked to newspapers in the U.S.) go through the motions of pretending to monitor the bank accounts of suspected terrorists, or those companies or individuals suspected of financing suspected terrorists. But nothing ever really comes of it.

And how could it? The Saudi government is one of the great enemies of Israel, so why should it expect its own citizens to oppose terrorism? I learned it from you, Dad! Those citizens probably think they are doing exactly what their government wants them to do.

37. They're brutal in the way they put down demonstrations of political expression.

Saudi Arabia is one of the most repressive regimes in the world—there is simply no question about it. In 1987, Saudi security forces clashed with Iranian pilgrims to Mecca, and 402 pilgrims died as a result. No one can organize a political demonstration in Saudi Arabia without governmental permission, although sometimes the line is not clear. Some demonstrations, especially anti-U.S. demonstrations organized by those holiest of holy clerics, are allowed to go on full force, because the government tacitly approves of them, or at least is placating the religious fanatics.

Meanwhile, unemployment is at or near an all-time high, around 25%, and the state-run oil company is laced with corruption and mismanagement, like most state-run enterprises (Isn't that the purpose?). The government keeps spending money they don't have, and the average person keeps getting poorer and poorer. But at least they have their religion to comfort them. It's funny, though, how when people get hungry, they can quickly modify their support for even the most fanatical religious regime. Especially after they have absorbed a few episodes of good old mindless American TV programs!

38. They come up with the same phony peace plan every few years.

Trade land for peace, and everything will be rosy! Just give up the lands you seized while defending yourself in the Six-Day War, Israel, and everyone will be happy. Never mind that we (the brotherhood of Egypt, Jordan, Syria, and us in Saudi Arabia back behind them) were about to attack you, and that we would do it again in a heartbeat if we thought you were vulnerable, and we wouldn't get our asses kicked. Fogetaboutit! Just roll over and play dead. We'll even promise to recognize you before we destroy you!

Ahem. Hypocrisy, and lying, and conniving, and so forth and so on, are supposed to be banned by all religions. But apparently not in this case. Anyway, this just isn't likely to happen anytime soon. The Saudi leaders hate the Israelis. The Saudi people hate them even more, probably based upon the bullshit of their leaders throughout all of the last century or more. It's a vicious circle, man! And it won't get any better until intolerant religions get softened up and begin to be corrupted a little from within. American television beamed in will do the job over time. It's already starting to happen in some of the Islamic countries, and things change faster and faster all the time.

39. They eat their own boogers.

Well, if you lived out in the extreme desert, wouldn't you? Or at least, do you know that you wouldn't?

Actually, there is no documented evidence that they do, or even that any single member of the family does. But it sounds like something they might do, doesn't it? Can you keep on being different, and yet not do some things that somebody else might find offensive? And which is more offensive, eating a booger (one's own), or discriminating against, and oppressing, women. Tough choice in today's times, isn't it? (Say, is this a plea for tolerance, or a summary of reasons not to kill the Saudi Royal Family, anyway?)

Even if they do do that, no matter how gross it sounds, if they're not harming anyone else, what difference does it make? Maybe it will take their mind off of terrorism for a while—or even permanently, if they're crusty enough.

40. They support the right of Israel to exist.

This one is a criticism from the Islamic point of view. But they really don't have to worry. There is no way in any kind of Hell that the Saudi Royal Family supports the right of Israel to exist, although they may have some mixed views on the subject. They hate the Jews, as almost everyone over there does, and they hated the Jews even before Israel was a state. And if they're going to retain power, they have to toe the line of the clerics whom they prop up with their subsidies.

On the other hand, if the state of Israel were to vanish, what then? Whom would they hate then? More importantly, whom would the Saudi Royal Family cast as the chief villain in order to galvanize the public and divert their attention away from the sorry state of affairs in Saudi Arabia? Without Israel, U.S. interests would wane somewhat in that region, and then who would stop the next Saddam Hussein when he goes into aggressive mode?

So, to all of you fundamentalist Muslim clerics out there, you don't have to worry on this one. But then, you already knew that, didn't you?

41. They want to normalize relations with Israel.

Well now, not really. But hey, if it keeps the U.S. happy during the period of tension following September 11, why not float the proposal? The fact that their own radical clerics don't even protest shows that the offer is not a sincere one, and that that fact is widely known in Saudi Arabia. But the U.S. is demanding that the Saudis make a good show of cooperation in the Arab-Israeli conflict, and this is one way they can do it without it costing them anything.

After all, there are enough hard-liners in Saudi Arabia and other Middle Eastern countries to sandbag any type of agreement. And of course, all Israel has to do is to give back the land it won defending itself. It has been attacked or blockaded numerous times since 1948, yet Israel must be content to fight a purely defensive war against aggressors on all sides. It hardly seems fair, does it? Well, you know something? It ain't.

42. They don't allow public displays of other religions.

Of course, this isn't totally unique, as other societies do this as well. However, probably none enforce it as thoroughly as does Saudi Arabia (especially now that the Taliban has been overthrown). It is simply another example of their overall harsh intolerance of anything different, based upon and justified by their religious beliefs. They say that Muhammad said that very thing, so therefore it must be done that way some fifteen centuries later. It's always interesting how religions lock people into stuff that supposedly happened more than a thousand years ago, as if there is no dispute that it really happened that way, when we can't even determine with certainty things that happened yesterday, or even hours ago.

However, it becomes more and more difficult to shield an entire population from the outside world. Perhaps what we need are tabloids for the theocracies, to show their people how their leaders (even their clergy) behave while outside of the country (and probably even in it, behind closed doors). Then the harshness of the restrictive rules could be softened and modernized. Usually, when people realize how many other people are doing the same thing, they become more accepting of other things, and may even try one or more of those things themselves.

43. They don't allow immigrant workers of different religions to be buried there.

This is an interesting one, and it is kind of linked to the one just above about displays of other religions. If an immigrant worker from another country dies there, the body has to be flown or otherwise shipped out of the country for burial. Muhammad said so, back in the 600's. Therefore, we have to do it that way. Now, if only I could convince people that I'm a prophet . . .

Interestingly, polls show that the Islamic world likes American culture (TV, rock music, cigarettes) in great numbers, even a majority in some Islamic countries. There's just the little matter of our policy towards Israel.

44. They just don't "do the right thing."

I wonder if any of them have even read Albert Jay Nock's famous essay, *On Doing the Right Thing*. If not, then perhaps they should. Then maybe their country and the world would be a better place. Right now, they base everything on the Koran, as if any one book could provide guidance in all areas of life.

And even their devotion to the Koran is subject to suspicion and interpretation. It seems they only follow it to the extent necessary to appease the public in Saudi Arabia. Once they leave there and come to America, or to Europe, many of the ones not in public life strip off their traditional Muslim clothing and wear Western clothing. They listen to rock music, or even old Frank Sinatra tapes, and they watch all kinds of TV shows and read some risqué books. Some of them may even say "Goddamn" or "Fuck."

45. They go through a show of pretending to "lighten up" on dissidents.

Every so often, the Saudi Royal Family seems to go easy on critics of the regime, and that usually gets some play in the media. But, when you look closer, it turns out that the dissidents they are going easy on are the religious fanatics who probably represent the majority of the country, and who have criticized the regime for not being rabidly religious enough, and for not trying hard enough to destroy Israel. This is one of the consequences the Saudi Royal Family faces as a result of keeping its subjects poor, and trying to tranquilize them through religious indoctrination. Religious fanatics turn on you with a fury once they get some broad support.

But the true measure of whether a regime really supports and/ or tolerates the rights of dissidents lies in whether they allow the freedom of speech and expression of those who express a minority point of view, not the majority point of view. When has the Saudi regime ever allowed to be heard the voices of gay rights? Free market economics? A national lottery? Soft porn on cable? Abortion on demand? Greater rights for other religions?

It simply won't happen. If they allow some dissident religious fanatics to speak out without fear of arrest, it is a strategy to placate their enemies, to let them let off steam and get it out of their system. They do this in order to prevent a massive revolt that could bring down the entire system, and their entire way of life. Once their world begins to crumble, there will be no end to it. Even if they flee the country, their assets will be subject to lawsuits and seizure the world round. And they know it. That is why they adopt some seemingly peculiar strategies to secure their bases.

But don't ever mistake it for true liberalism.

46. They really want to live life in the fast lane, while pretending to support religion.

This one I think we can safely agree on, at least with regard to some of the members. The people of Saudi Arabia are only a means to an end, providing the revenue and the labor supply to keep the Kingdom afloat and operating. And when a high-flying family desires to remain in power, they must placate the masses. Give them all the religion they want, every day, and two-for-one specials on weekends. Give them what it takes to keep them calm and in a non-protesting mood. And if they protest, then allow them a little protesting (Hell, they're your paid employees, the clerics), but not too much.

If you give them all the religion they want, you can keep them poor and subservient, especially if you can get yourself identified as being on some par with the Almighty. It's been done since the beginning of time, and it may be the best system for today's time in Saudi Arabia. Who knows for certain?

47. They make people feel that we should "Kill 'em all and let God sort 'em out."

This is one of the unfortunate side effects of the Islamic-Christian-Jewish, etc. controversies. One thing leads to another, and then prejudice begets prejudice. The more prejudiced one becomes, the more the hatred boils over at the slightest provocation or opportunity. Then the cycle rushes furiously round and round, until finally some temporary moment of sanity brings the cycle to a standstill, or at least a slowdown. One group feeds off of the prejudices and hatred of another, and then aims their own prejudices and hatred back at the same group, or even off in the direction of another group, and so forth and so on.

Then someone thinks, "Kill 'em all and let God sort 'em out." But we can hardly blame the Saudi Royalty Family for that. They definitely fan the flames here and there, but they do so mainly to hang on to their power and privileged positions.

48. They ran like scared rabbits after Saddam Hussein invaded Kuwait.

Well, that isn't quite true. They actually didn't need to run, because the U.S. came to their rescue. But you can bet that they would have packed up and left in a hurry if the Good Ole USA had not come to their defense. The heck with what the rest of the Arab world thought; they would not have sacrificed their lifestyle by staying and fighting. If so, they would never have asked the U.S. to come into their territory and fight their fight for them, especially when so many of their fanatical countrymen were against it, and aghast at it.

Recently, they were back in Saddam's corner, afraid to criticize him, toeing his line as if nothing ever happened. But back in 1990, he wanted their oil, and he wanted their heads on a platter, and maybe their shanks, too—just like their good friend Idi Amin would like his enemies!

Of course, at that time, the U.S. had its motives as well, but without Saudi permission, it never would have happened. Funny how it all works out, huh?

49. They have always let the other Arab states do their dirty work.

There is a lot to say for this one, especially as far as military action against Israel is concerned. They definitely let Egypt, Jordan, and Syria shoulder the burden in the 50s, 60s, and 70s. Nothing much happened in the 1980s, although Israel attacked Lebanon, and the Palestinian terrorists stepped up their activity.

Then, in 1990, Iraq attacked Kuwait, and everybody thought that Saudi Arabia was next. But was Saudi Arabia ready to fight to defend its honor? Apparently not, because then we went in and did their dirty work for them. It was the height of naiveté for us to do that, and then expect that our efforts were going to be appreciated. When has that ever happened? An argument could be made that we should have sat back and let Saddam crush them like the grapes of a good Cabernet. After all, could he really have been any worse? At least he was less subtle, and his intentions were easier to detect.

How they have convinced the other Arab states to act militarily against Israel without themselves getting involved militarily is anybody's guess. Egypt and Jordan, and possible Syria, have now wised up, so what the future will hold is uncertain at this point.

50. They won't allow children who have been taken from their mothers in America to leave.

This one is especially heinous. If a Saudi male has children by a woman from another country, then kidnaps them and takes them to Saudi Arabia, the Saudi government will not let them leave without permission. They are forcibly converted to Islam (nothing like forcing somebody to believe something! Bet you get a great commitment out of that!) and held against their will. If the mothers are allowed to see the children at all, it is only if the government allows it.

This shows the horror that develops when a religion dominates a society so completely. People tend to need the religion to comfort themselves, and give some kind of meaning to their (seemingly) otherwise meaningless lives. Once people need that kind of strict crutch, then the most consistent and strict proponents of that religion keep the masses in line through a guilt methodology. If you don't do this and that, then you're not a good Muslim (in this case). Therefore, people tend to go along with the strict construction set forth by the most extreme elements.

51. They allow the U.S. to influence their policies.

Another criticism from the radical Islamic point of view. Well, they are politicians, and politics makes—well, you know the old line. There is no doubt that U.S. oil interests and the Saudis have some of the same goals, and otherwise conflicting forces do get together and cooperate from time to time. So there are some legitimate disagreements between the Saudi Royal Family and the radical fundamentalists who comprise such a major force in the country.

In a way, one could almost make a bare case that the Saudi Royal Family is trying to lead the country, and maybe the entire Arab world, out of the clutches of the radical Islamic grip in which it has languished for so long. But that would be too easy, and also incorrect. It is probably more accurate to say that the Saudi Royal Family's very survival depends on it trying to appease several very powerful conflicting interests, including, but not limited to, the U.S. government, the radical Islamic fundamentalists, and the poor, barely surviving masses. The latter group is not yet organized as an effective, political force; it will probably take a very violent revolution in the country to give them the power they need.

52. They arrest some alleged terrorists every now and then, and then slap them on the wrists.

Every now and then, the Saudis go through a show of arresting some Islamic radicals, then later either let them go, or slap them on the wrists with relatively light sentences. This is one of their ways of seeming to cooperate with the U.S. in the war on terrorism, but actually it is insignificant in that fight. It is really more of a way of staying on the good side of the U.S., and coming across as a moderate force in the region. At the same time, however, there is an understanding between the Saudi government and the Islamic radicals that they have to do this every once in a while in order to gain as many concessions out of the U.S. as they can.

Although the gesture is usually not actually a sincere one, it still causes some hatred from the most radical elements of the Islamic fundamentalist movement, and so they feel the heat from the other direction as well.

53. They arrest radicals to appease the U.S. government.

In order to stay in good with the U.S. government, they periodically arrest Islamic radicals. This is similar to other policies the Saudis use to straddle the fence between radical Islam and Western modernism. Maybe one can't really blame them, as there are camps of both sorts in Saudi Arabia, and indeed throughout the Islamic world. Once they have been exposed to TV, alcohol, pornography, gambling, birth control, and midget wrestling, it's kind of hard for them to turn back to fundamentalist religion.

But there are those, as there are in most countries, who want to impose their fundamentalist views on others. Some of those individuals may really believe the entire package—hook, line and sinker—but others may just be using it to mask some personal or psychological problems. Tomorrow those latter folks could be Marxists or rattlesnake handlers, but today they are fundamentalist Muslims.

The Saudi Royal Family has to deal with these diverse groups of people, and with many variations within those strains, if they want to hold onto their power and money, and it is not easy.

54. They support Wahhabiism.

What's that? They do? Well, let's kill 'em all right away, then. Well, now, wait a minute! Hold your horses! Admittedly, it does sound funny. It even may sound like a variety of terrorism (Some would say they go hand in hand.). But actually Wahhabiism is a sect of Islam that advocates strict adherence to the Koran. Nothing necessarily bad in that, as long as it allows for others to have the freedom to practice their own religion(s), or lack thereof, which I doubt that it does.

It does have a funny sound. It's the kind of name that might provoke a school bully to pick on someone who practiced it, or to cause one to throw rocks at adherents of it who rode a bicycle through the neighborhood. But it does actually exist, and the Saudis do practice it, and actively push its growth.

55. They give sanctuary to Idi Amin in their country.

This one is a good one! Idi Amin, the former dictator of Uganda, who slaughtered and practiced cannibalism on his own people while ruling his country in the 1970s, is allowed to live in Saudi Arabia with whatever wealth he spirited out of Uganda when he fled there more than twenty years ago.

Amin took power in 1971 and started a reign of terror in Uganda that ended only when he fled in about 1979. He had ventured outside his own country to attack Tanzania, and in a classic turnabout-is-fair-play example, Tanzania kicked his ass, and he had no choice but to run like a scared rabbit. But before that all happened, he had killed more than 100,000 of Uganda's own citizens, he had allowed the hijackers of an Israeli airliner to take refuge in Uganda (Remember the heroic "Raid on Entebbe"?), the economy had collapsed, and he had engaged in a feast of cannibalism.

The cannibalism is what sets him apart from so many other dictators (although at least one other African dictator, in the Central African Republic, also feasted on his own citizens). Remember the famous quote from Idi Amin: "I love Americans! I had three for breakfast this morning!" And also remember that story (It's just strange enough to be true!) about how he was entertaining some visiting dignitaries at a state dinner, and after they had eaten, he announced that they had just feasted on one of his principal adversaries (make that former principal adversaries!).

And this is the man Saudi Arabia allows to take refuge in their pitiful country.

56. They tolerate bombings of non-Muslim residents by fanatical dissidents.

A while back, some British citizens were killed with car and parcel bombs. A round of bombings against British and American citizens occurred in 2000 and 2001. But instead of locking up Saudi dissidents responsible for the bombings, the Saudi government locked up other British citizens and tortured confessions out of them! The Saudi Royal Family really is a pitiful, Nazi-like establishment!

They don't want to admit that there are dissidents, and plenty of them, in their country, composed of their own people. They didn't even want to admit that most of the 9/11 hijackers came from their country, or that al Qaeda operates in their country. Denial, denial, denial. Maybe they should make O.J. an honorary Saudi.

It is true that most of the dissidents are anti-U.S., and are fanatical Muslims. Or are they? As I mentioned earlier, those are the dissidents they allow, because those dissidents are the most powerful, or maybe the most vocal, and they try to pacify them in a strategic way. But couldn't there be plenty of dissidents who believe in other religions, or maybe even no religion at all, and who like the U.S. and the Western lifestyle with all its "decadence"? Very possible.

57. They hold the children of any Saudi who flees there from another country, even if he is legally married and the spouse has a right to have the children visit her.

Yes, they do. If a Saudi marries a citizen of another country and they have children, and he (the Saudi citizen) then decides to return to Saudi Arabia, then the Saudi government will allow the Saudi citizen to hold those children, no matter the circumstances. This happens even if the husband is already married to another woman, and even if the child is sodomized! Isn't religion great???

Such horror stories are fairly commonplace, and the rest of the world tolerates it. By the way, the children cannot leave even once they become adults, and even if their Saudi relatives freely come and go. It is all part of the whole Saudi way of dissing other religions besides Islam. And they believe that the U.S. government will do nothing, because of our interests in Saudi oil, and because we perceive them to be moderates in the region.

By the way, this is not the same as Reason Number 50—you just thought it was!

58. They own racehorses and other expensive stuff while their own people are starving.

This one is definitely true. In fact, recently a Saudi prince was killed while on the way to the place where he stored his racehorses (I wonder what Racehorse Haynes would think of that!). They truly do flaunt their wealth, even while millions of poor people in their country suffer. They seem to think nothing of the contradiction, and keep doing things as they have always done, only more so.

The children are even more spoiled than the parents, as most children who inherit wealth are. Sometimes they do give to charity, but only after ensuring that the mass of people stay poor, by giving them little or no opportunity to prosper in the Saudi economy. Very rarely does a rich person, even among the most liberal ones, care so much about starvation and poverty that they give their entire inherited fortune away, or even give it down to an upper middle income level. It just doesn't happen. And if starvation and poverty bothered them that much, you would think they would. After all, it literally could save many lives!

59. They tried to keep the U.S. from invading and overthrowing Saddam Hussein.

After the U.S. saved the Saudis in 1991 following the Iraqi invasion of Kuwait, the Saudis quickly forgot how much trouble they had been in, and that the U.S. had been their primary defender. Or maybe the Saudi Royal Family just couldn't admit to their own people that "The Great Satan" was good for something besides watching decadent soap operas and drinking alcohol. At any rate, here we are, more than ten years later, and they still feebly protested any attack on Iraq to depose Saddam Hussein.

The former head of the Saudi external intelligence service, Prince Turki al-Faisal (sounds familiar—and they talk about inbreeding in Mississippi!), said a while back that the Saudis had passed along intelligence to the U.S. in the past about opposition within Iraq that might have been useful in deposing Saddam Hussein, but that the Saudis had become convinced that the U.S. wasn't serious about it. And he linked the whole idea, about invading Iraq, to a pre-condition: that the Israelis give in to Palestinian demands. Surprise, Surprise, Sergeant!

60. They cooperated with the "devils" in the CIA to try to capture Osama bin Laden.

Yes, it's definitely true. In fact, the very same former external intelligence service chief mentioned above, Prince Turki al-Faisal (say, are any of these princes related to the esteemed sports announcer, Bob Prince, by any chance?) acknowledges that he worked closely with the CIA to try to capture bin Laden in the late 1990s. As another part of the ongoing, never-ceasing delicate balancing act performed by the Saudi Royal Family, they try to appease the U.S. in catching an Islamic hard-liner, even while they are promoting a very strict version of Islam within their own borders.

You would think one side or the other would wake up to this duplicity, and in fact both sides are. Many Americans, especially since 9/11, are asking why anyone would support a country that recognized the Taliban, produces some of the most hard-line Islamic nuts, produced Osama bin Laden, hates Israel with as much fervor as any other nation in the Islamic world (and they don't hate them so much for their dispute with the Palestinians—they hate them because they are Jewish), acted cowardly in the face of Saddam Hussein (who probably could have wiped the floor with the lot of them), and are just plain intolerant. And many hard-line fundamentalist Muslims are asking why they should tolerate anybody who deals with Americans, and who only sponsors terrorism when they think no one respectable is looking.

61. They don't allow importation of goods made in Israel.

Yes, they even blacklist companies that import goods into the country using fake certificates of origin to try to get around the discriminatory laws. They are so blinded by their hatred of the Jews that they won't even allow Jewish goods into the country. It makes you wonder whether they would even allow a Jewish doctor to operate on them if it would save their lives. The answer to that is: of course they would, especially if they could do it in the U.S., out of earshot of their own countrymen.

What a silly policy, that they would not care about the quality of goods, but only the religion of the people who made them. How much more short-sighted and ignorant can one get? And how much more hypocritical? Because it is obvious that when they enjoy their somehow-gotten wealth in other countries around the globe (usually a wealthy or resort area), they don't give a hootin' hell (as Major Kong would say) who provides the goods and/or services.

62. They waffled about allowing the U.S. to use military bases in the country to attack Iraq.

Well, maybe you can't blame them on this one. After all, surely it was and is a valid question—whether we should have attacked Iraq or not? And surely any other country has sovereignty over its own lands. And we know that the Saudis love peace more than anything.

However, they did call us in to save their bacon (even though they don't eat it) when Saddam Hussein attacked Kuwait, and the general feeling was that he was going to attack Saudi Arabia next. As I've said before, if Israel didn't exist, many of the Islamic countries would be fighting each other. Not necessarily because they are Islamic, but because of the militaristic governmental structure in many countries, and the "Royal" structure in others. It's a real recipe for war and mass destruction and loss of life.

It's much easier to destroy than to create, and it's much easier to fight than to live in peace. Religion must be compromised if the peoples of the earth are not going to destroy each other.

63. They cooperate with the U.S. in fighting terrorism.

While this may seem to be a contradictory criticism, it is actually true. They do indeed cooperate with the U.S. in fighting terrorism—they just do it at their convenience. If I were an Islamic militant (not quite the beat of *If I Were a Rich Man*), this one would really piss me off. Fortunately, I'm not, so I can examine it objectively. And the fact is that the Saudis interrogate terrorists quite often, and sometimes they pass on what they learn to the U.S.

It's all part of the delicate balance in the Middle East. After all, even Libya cooperates with us when it suits their purpose, and we bombed the shit out of them, and even killed the Great Man's son. However, that was then, and this is now.

At any rate, the Saudis are helping. Bless their little hearts. Rock n' Roll. Over the dunes and through the sand, to Grandmother's house we go.

By the way, this is a fundamentalist complaint.

64. They don't really give much of a shit about the Palestinians.

This is true, and it is the ultimate in hypocrisy. They have never offered the Palestinians citizenship, and they have never even allowed refugee camps in Saudi Arabia. The UN Relief and Works Agency (UNRWA), which is supposed to help the Palestinians, is poorly funded. All of the Arab states together contribute under 2% of the total funding. Saudi Arabia contributes very little, in spite of raising a lot of money to give to the Palestinian authorities for their own purposes.

In spite of all the talk about Arab brotherhood, it amounts to about the same as talk about most forms of "brotherhood." As soon as no one is directly looking, the brotherhood divides, as many segments seek to maximize their own agenda.

It goes back to one thing: if they didn't have Israel to rally against, they would be fighting each other. As recent history has shown, they often fight each other even though Israel *is* around, and they kill each other in much greater numbers.

65. They paid off Osama bin Laden to keep him from attacking Saudi Arabia.

Yes, there seems to be some evidence of this, although it is far from certain. But it makes sense. When did the Saudis ever attack Israel? Defend Kuwait? The Saudi method is to run from trouble, or to buy it off. Have your enemy point in another direction, perhaps even towards the Good Ole USA.

Most people in Saudi Arabia support bin Laden and his efforts, just like most people in the South at one time supported slavery, then Jim Crow, and maybe even lynching, if they were necessary to keep the prevailing system intact. In Saudi Arabia, the prevailing system is fundamentalism. As I have mentioned many times, the Saudi Royal family is walking that delicate tightrope, kind of like the late Shah of Iran (remember him?).

So they possibly pay off bin Laden, and instead of being diverted in several directions, he focuses on his main enemy (the U.S.). Thanks for nuthin', guys!

66. They periodically threaten to cut off oil if we don't change our Middle Eastern policy.

Yes, they do, too. I can hear you now, saying, "But they promised not to use oil as a weapon." Yeah. And Nixon said we wouldn't have him to kick around anymore. Well, it is so that they have and do threaten to cut off oil. But so what? They can't eat it or drink it, and their religion forbids them from fucking it. So they have to sell it to us, or we will just buy it from somewhere else. Plus, oil is so fungible, if you will, that the oil we buy from someone else could be the same oil that the Saudis sold to someone else. We are becoming less dependent on Saudi oil, and if the price of oil rises far enough, we'll become less dependent on oil. There are always a host of technological innovations on the shelf, waiting for market conditions to ripen for them to come into wide usage. We use oil because it is still the cheapest. We used whale oil at one time. Maybe in the future we'll use quail dung. The point is: we are *not* really dependent on Saudi oil—and they know it.

UNCLAIMED BAGGAGE

67. They haven't even claimed the remains of their own terrorist citizens.

As widely noted right after the 9/11 attacks, most of the hijackers were Saudi Arabian citizens. The Saudi government denied this at first, of course, saying that the hijackers had merely faked their identities. Then they tried to say that the hijackers were trying to drive a wedge between Saudi Arabia and the U.S. At least they have finally acknowledged the obvious.

Now it comes to light that no one has stepped forward to claim the remains of the nine hijackers who have been identified (Those are the four on the flight that crashed in Pennsylvania, and the five who crashed into the Pentagon—the remains of the ten who crashed into the World Trade Center towers have not been identified at the time of this writing.). The Saudi Arabian government has not even come forward to claim the remains of its own citizens, even though its own alleged financing of terrorist activities may have had an indirect effect on the events.

Here's a practical suggestion. Since the Saudis see fit to give sanctuary to Idi Amin, the cannibal and former dictator of Uganda (and one of the greatest mass murderers of the 20th Century), I propose that we send the remains back to Saudi Arabia, on the condition that they be used as a meal for Amin. I don't know if he likes his terrorists well-done or not, but I'm sure he would give it a shot at least.

I still find it unbelievable that anyone would give sanctuary to a cannibal and mass murderer, just because he hated Jews. Yet that is exactly what the Saudis have done. What a great, noble, moral, religious stance!

68. They periodically attack Christians in other countries.

Hard to believe, isn't it? And maybe they have a point here. After all, Christian fundamentalism can be just as dangerous as Islamic fundamentalism, or indeed fundamentalism in any religion. It would seem so simple for those who believe in a particular religion to live by example, and thereby win converts to their cause by showing potential converts their happiness and success in life— success by however one would measure it. But that is too simple. And of course, the Saudi Royal Family doesn't really believe in that, anyway.

So what does the Saudi Royal Family really believe in? Do they really believe in Islam of the kind we associate with Saudi Arabia? Some fundamentalists would doubt that very seriously, saying that they only pay lip service to it in order to maintain power. If so, what is their goal? To put one over on all their countrymen by stealth? To fool all of the people all of the time?

Or is it to bring them forward into modern times, but also by stealth? Elevate their countrymen and water down that fundamentalism over time, so that one day the country will join the enlightened?

Who knows, but right now they are making enemies across the whole world spectrum.

69. They "respect" women to the point of death.

We know they repress women; that's a given. But just how far they (or at least their followers) will go is sometimes shocking. In March 2002, approximately 14 girls died while trying to escape a fire at a school in Saudi Arabia. Members of a fundamentalist group supposedly interfered with the rescue, because the female students trying to escape were not wearing the proper clothing to appear outside. In other words, while they were fleeing the blaze and trying to stay alive, they were not wearing the proper headwear and neckwear to cover themselves in public, and when they emerged, they would have been dressed improperly. So they died instead.

It's nice to have other people looking out for your interests, and your soul. Some people just love you to death for your own benefit. It is fair to mention, however, that this did not directly involve the Saudi Royal Family, but rather members of a group called (believe it or not!) the Committee for the Promotion of Virtue and the Prevention of Vice. Sounds like some of our own folks!

70. They don't want the U.S. to ram planes into their newly developed skyscrapers.

Recently, although not widely known in the West, two new skyscrapers have been developed in Riyadh, Saudi Arabia. Each was developed by a prince of the Saudi Royal Family.

First, and completed in May 2000, was the Al Faisaliah Center, developed by Prince Bandar bin Saud bin Khalid. It was 881 feet tall, and has a huge geodesic sphere on top containing a three-story restaurant.

The second one, completed in 2002 (but originally scheduled to be completed in September 2001), is the Kingdom Centre. It was a project developed by our old friend Prince Alwaleed ("Take my money if you will promise to hate the Jews") Bin Talal. It is 972 feet tall, and has a 60-meter skybridge across the top. It would be a perfect target for Osama bin Laden when he decides to really take on the Saudi Royal Family. But alas, they have already bought him off—paid him to attack others and leave them alone.

Of course, no sane person would wish it upon the people in Saudi Arabia for terrorists of any sort (and one thing we know is that terrorism is by no means limited to Arabs or Muslims) to destroy these fine buildings and the people in them. But it is said that the Saudi hierarchy is very nervous because of what happened on 9/11. And the entire Saudi Kingdom is a very vulnerable institution, subject to attack from many different sources, even insane Westerners (They can be the worst of all!).

71. They like the smell of their own farts.

Well, who doesn't? And what in the world is wrong with that???
Ahem . . .

Actually, there is no proof that that is true. It's not even certain whether a good blooper could even survive out in the Saudi desert any longer than a Muhammad Ali (no relation to "Chemical" Ali) left jab did in the ring. The hot, dry desert wind would carry it away like a hummingbird darting around the back yard. And the fumes from the numerous oil and chemical refineries would overpower the smell of even the most powerful fart.

Not that a little entertainment wouldn't be good for them. They need to loosen up, what with the stress of dealing with both the Islamic fundamentalists and the U.S. government (Just imagine if the U.S. people had as much say about it as they would like!).

Maybe one day they'll appreciate the finer things in life.

72. They think only Muslims can frighten people with devastating terrorist acts.

Well, we don't really know whether they think that or not, but sometimes it seems like they do. But that is a trap that even many Americans fall into, but for different reasons. The notion of people unafraid to commit suicide is really only one step removed from heroic efforts undertaken in the heat of battle, and there have always been people of many stripes who were not afraid to give their own life for a cause. Yet we have treated the Muslim suicides as something vastly different. They don't have powerful armies, so they strike at civilians to get what they want, and they strike in as devastating a way as they can. Sometimes they succeed.

But wait a minute. Some years ago, the Japanese did the same thing near the end of World War II, in desperation. A few years ago, Timothy McVeigh bombed a building and killed many people. We thought it was an Islamic fundamentalist at first, but now we know better. McVeigh was certainly willing to give his own life. He only hung around in order to try to make a political defense at his trial, and when that failed, he gave up and cheerfully made himself a martyr to his cause.

Airplanes. The terrorists seem to like airplanes. Large numbers of people. Easy to get onto and take over. Now they can even fly them into buildings, maybe even nuclear reactors, greatly expanding the damage they can cause.

Now, let's say a Timothy McVeigh mentality starts to set in with airline pilots. Those guys are unionized, and they tend to think alike. A very high proportion of them in the U.S. are white guys. Ex-military. Sullen. Life has been turning around on them. They don't like those other people trying to get into the cockpit.

Women. African-Americans. Maybe some gays. They're angry as hell. But they're Americans first.

All of a sudden, they decide to take their revenge and drive their airplanes into something. Mecca? Downtown Riyadh? It could happen—soon.

I think we'd better start thinking about how to keep kooks off airplanes. It may be more important than anthrax or smallpox or poison gas.

73. They push for an increase in oil production against the interests of other OPEC members.

We do our best to be fair to all viewpoints.

Yes, it's true. The Saudis secretly, or sometimes even openly, push for an increase in oil production, which would obviously cause the price of oil to stay the same against rising demand, or even fall if production is increased enough. All of that helps the U.S. economy, and the economy of the entire oil-dependent industrialized world, especially the "First World" countries that have a high standard of living.

Who knows? One of these days, cheap oil prices may even benefit the Saudis. After all, it is usually a bad sign when a country is so dependent on a natural resource, like oil, diamonds, sulfur, etc. They usually put their energies into maintaining the worldwide value of that resource, even at the expense of developing their economies in other directions, and letting market forces operate so that there is more diversity and a greater standard of living. Contrast wealthy countries like the U.S., the Western European countries, Japan, and Hong Kong, with Third World countries like South Africa, Louisiana, Venezuela, and yes, Saudi Arabia. That comparison speaks volumes.

74. They pretend to their subjects not to help the U.S. on terrorism while actually doing so.

A while back, the Saudi government acted surprised when the U.S. moved to freeze the assets of a prominent Saudi citizen, Wael Julaidan, who was associated with Saudi Arabian charities. However, at the same time, the Saudi government, through its permanent representative to the United Nations, Fawzi A. Shobokshi, advised the UN Security Council's terrorism-finance committee that Mr. Julaidan should be added to the committee's list of individuals who fund terrorism.

This is yet another example of the Saudi Royal Family's infamous duplicity. However, they are not the only ones who act in such a manner. It is almost routine practice for those who run governments around the world to act in other than a straightforward manner. It is almost as if a requirement to be an important participant in running a government is to have the attitude that the citizens must be fooled, or at least their intelligence must be tested (or perhaps insulted!).

What, then is the ultimate goal of the Saudi Royal Family? To survive?

Who will be left at the end? And what will remain of them???

75. They don't even have a proper and orderly succession plan.

This is true. The ailing King Fahd may name whomever he wants, without regard to fairness or relation. Some would say that this is power at its worst, while others would argue that there are much worse things.

Right now, the battle could be between 78 year-old Crown Prince Abdullah and 74 year-old Prince Sultan, Defense Minister and father of the Saudi ambassador to Washington, Prince Bandar. If that sounds like a current battle for the Republican presidential nomination between Ronald Reagan and Barry Goldwater's ghost, then maybe there is a good reason for that.

The two princes have blown hot and cold on the U.S., aid to terrorists, Israel—all the hot-button issues in the Middle East— and even on the issue of the deeply ingrained corruption that affects all members of the Saudi Royal Family. The family is very corrupt, so much so that it is simply accepted there as a law of nature, much like the law of gravity or Newton's Laws of Motion. Some say the family has enriched itself by as much as $50 *billion* over the years through kickbacks for government contracts.

Meanwhile, the economy is very stagnant, poverty is rampant among the masses, and discontent grows faster with each passing year.

76. They won't let U.S. oil and gas companies have access to Saudi Arabia's most promising natural gas fields.

After negotiating with American and European oil companies, the Saudis seemed to reverse themselves, and continue to forbid those companies from drilling for gas. The Saudis have offered lesser fields to the foreign companies, but the rate of return would be lower than on the larger fields. Apparently, the Saudi Royal Family wants to keep its stranglehold on the Saudi economy, with most of the benefits going back into the family. Saudi Arabia has produced all of its own oil and gas since the 1970s.

This plays right into the hands of the fundamentalists who oppose any U.S., and probably any non-Islamic, presence in Saudi Arabia. They are, after all, opposed to any military, economic, and cultural presence by non-Islamic powers. Meanwhile the economy sputters, and the masses go hungry. The whole purpose of the initiative (to allow foreign companies to drill for gas) was to jump-start the long-ailing economy, but that will have to take a back seat to religious fanaticism, as well as to the greedy interests of those in power.

The Saudis are badly mistaken, however, if they think that the U.S. "dependence" on oil can be pushed past a certain point. If the U.S is "dependent" on oil, it is because oil is still the cheapest solution. When it no longer is, oil will cease to have the value it has today. The Saudis know this, having gotten greedy before, but they probably have to relearn the lesson from time to time.

77. They openly criticized Saddam Hussein.

Well, some of them did, at least in America. Prince Bandar, the Saudi ambassador to the U.S., is well known for his open criticisms of Saddam Hussein. He basically called him a madman, and a liar, and a propagandist (is that bad?), and further said that he would put nothing past him. Whether he said such things as openly back home in Saudi Arabia is another matter.

Saudi Arabia had good reason to fear Saddam Hussein; at least, the Saudi Royal Family did. Saddam didn't seem to like royal families of either Arab or non-Arab background. His contempt for the Kuwaiti Royal Family was evident, and his contempt for the Saudi Royal Family was only one step behind.

It was clear that, if Saddam were to be deposed, or at least, if Iraqi oil began to flow to the full extent that it could, the Saudis would be impacted in a negative way: Saudi Arabia's share of world oil production would drop, and relationships with the Saudis would be less important (although still important). However, to have allowed Saddam to stick around frightened everyone who thought about him, even many who hate the U.S.

Nobody knew how to deal with a fundamentalist like Saddam Hussein; he showed that in his war with Iran, and by the way he handled dissidents in his own country. And he knew that they posed a great danger to him as well. Any man who had at least three doubles who appeared in his place in public was looking out for himself!

78. They even admit to their own corruption.

Prince Bandar, the Saudi ambassador to the U.S., was quoted a while back as saying that the Saudi Royal Family had received enormous sums in kickbacks over the years. However, he didn't say precisely that. He said that Saudi Arabia's modernization had cost quite a bit more than it might otherwise have cost if there were no corruption there. But he didn't say that the family had received all of that money. Instead, he implied that perhaps the country had paid more than it should have because of corruption. There is a little difference between the two things.

And is Saudi Arabia any more or less corrupt than any other Third World Country? We mentioned Louisiana earlier—plenty of corruption there. Libya? Mexico? Bolivia? We could go on and on, but the list would be endless. No need to put the Saudis in a special category. Pick up any newspaper in the U.S. on any day, and you will read about corruption—past, present, alleged and proven. It will happen as long as governments have money to disburse, and goods and services it needs to purchase with that money.

79. They set up web sites, and run television and newspaper advertisements, promoting the family.

Well, yes, they do—or at least others do it for them. But they are, after all, a business, and that's pretty much it. They may perform some other activities, like all prominent families, but just as in those cases, their motives may be traced back to a desire to maximize the family's psychic income, which may of course be different at times from purely monetary income. So it is not surprising that they would toot their own horn, and that they would try to do it somewhat quietly, intelligently, without the listener or the reader (or the surfer) being aware that propaganda is going on.

Let's face it—it would take a lot of killing to dispose of everyone who does many of the things that the Saudi Royal Family does. Too many of the things they do are simply part of a pattern of prominent, wealthy, old families. One would have to be more discriminating than that to come up with a reason that has an aura of legitimacy.

But let's keep looking—we still have 22 reasons to go!

80. They don't like it when another Arab state liberalizes its policies.

Saudi Arabia has developed more and more friction with its next-door neighbor Qatar, another Wahhabi Islamic country like Saudi Arabia. In recent years, Qatar has greatly liberalized its policies (and its interpretations of Wahhabiism), and has begun allowing more freedom, including use and sale of alcohol, and freedom of expression beyond that ever known before. They also now allow women to drive, vote, and hold office, any of which would be heresy in Saudi Arabia, which sees itself as the standard-bearer of Wahhabiism.

As mentioned before, Wahhabiism is a super-fundamentalist strain of Islam, named after Mohammed ibn Abdel Wahhab, an 18th century preacher. The strict policies we all think of when we think of Islamic fundamentalism, such as women covering their faces (and everything else) in public, segregation of the sexes, and hostility towards other beliefs, have traditionally been cornerstones of this weird interpretation of Islam.

The Saudis run their country in that strict fashion, as noted many times before, and if another Arab state wants to liberalize, like Qatar, they wring their hands and get mad. Recently, they recalled their ambassador to Qatar because they didn't like the direction Qatar was headed on this.

81. They're very secretive about how succession to the crown is handled.

Yes, this is true, and it is yet another example of their anti-democratic philosophy. *They* know what is best for everyone else! Should you hate Israel and Jews? They'll tell you if you should, and how much to. Should you hate America? They'll tell you whether or not to do that, and to what degree. Should you mistreat your wife? They'll tell you what's OK and what's not.

Anyway, the succession process is secret, like so much else about the mysterious family. The crown does not pass to the eldest son (there are many "sons" floating around the desert), but rather to the one most able to handle the duties of the role, as determined by the Saudi Royal Family (or a "committee" within it). You can bet that the head man will be a man, old, staunchly traditionalist, and moderate by Middle Eastern standards (but still anti-Israel and anti-Jewish).

There may be some competition among various branches of the family, what with the many children produced through multiple wives (They'd better give up that stuff if they ever want to become our 51st state!), but you can bet that the ruling family member will always turn to one of his own when making important political appointments, or awarding government contracts. Essentially nepotism runs wild in the Saudi Arabian government and business world (Praise Allah that it's not, as many believe, a sexual practice!).

82. Murder is OK when you have good reason to do it.

False. Wrongo. Incorrectamundo. Sorry to burst your bubble, but murder is wrong under any circumstances. Period. End of discussion.

83. They equivocated on allowing the U.S. to use their territory to strike against Iraq.

This one may look a little familiar, but it is really a different position. Instead of staking out a clear-cut position, the Saudi Royal Family, master politicians that they are (at least in their neck of the woods), try to be all things to all people. It can't be done, however, and that is why so many want to do them harm (As I've pointed out immediately above, that's wrong!).

The Saudi Royal Family cannot be all things to all people for an indefinite period. Too much TV and radio have taken their toll, especially now that advocates of the various extremes (fundamentalism and—well, the other position) know what they have to do—take their case directly to the people in order to move the ball one direction or the other.

The Saudi Royal Family is looking a little insincere and hypocritical these days, as it struggles with the decisions it has made over a long period of time, when the world wasn't watching it as closely as it does now, and when outside communication wasn't as easily available to its citizens as it is today. How extremely harsh the world's retrospective view can be!

84. They even accept Osama bin Laden's sons when they are deported from other countries.

When other countries, such as Iran, find that one of Osama bin Laden's sons is in their possession, they usually move to deport them, at least while the heat from 9/11 is still on. And Saudi Arabia is one of the countries they deport them to. He has a bunch of sons, so they could be anywhere in the world at any given time. Like the children of the rich everywhere, they probably have attended the best schools and been well taken care of.

The Saudis look after their own, especially if they need to in order to placate the fundamentalists in their country. While bin Laden himself is officially exiled, his family members are free to return, which is a fair policy, and helps weaken the "guilt by association" element. But it does help re-emphasize the Islamic nature of the Saudi state, and how far the government will go in order to maintain that theocratic atmosphere.

If the people of Saudi Arabia could see how various members of the Saudi Royal Family live when they are outside the gaze of their Muslim countrymen, they would cry out for rebellion, even if they didn't dare go through with it. And if the Saudi Royal Family could do as it pleases, it would weaken the theocratic atmosphere and introduce a more secular air to the country. But they don't dare do that just yet; better to wait. Religion would survive under their preferred system, but it would be different from the present version. A rich person's religion can be far different from a poor person's.

85. They flaunt their wealth even while "helping" the poor.

Our old friend Prince Alwaleed bin Talal is one of the main offenders here, but he is certainly not the only one. It is a familiar scenario, not unknown in the U.S. as well: the wealthy and influential take steps, primarily through government, to limit competition and ensure that only they will accumulate wealth, and that the masses will stay poor. Then they make a production out of receiving the poor people and dispensing gifts to them, supposedly as acts of kindness. Of course, what it actually is is an act of psychological chicanery, a way of convincing the masses of poor folks that they are in fact being good to them, when in fact the very basic rules of the game are hopelessly stacked against them.

This goes on regularly in many Third World countries, and has for years. The Saudis have escaped coverage of that mainly because they have seemed like moderates among the Arab states in the Middle East. They haven't been as rabidly anti-Israel as Libya or Syria, for example, and they have seemed pro-U.S. on the surface, so the media has not really dug into their great division of wealth until recently. In fact, until recently, the media only seemed interested in their actions as they have related to the U.S. or Israel.

But Prince Alwaleed receives visitors at his desert tent and hears them plead for money, berate Jews and Americans (and perhaps other non-Muslims as well), and carries on in the grand way of the pre-arranged billionaire. But is there a storm brewing in the desert?

86. They try to slip "modernization" by the people.

Yes, indeed. If ever there was a paternalistic government, it is the one in Saudi Arabia. "We know what is best for you" seems to be their guiding philosophy (not that we don't have plenty like that in the Good Ole USA). But the Saudis are something else again. The people, at least many of them who are influenced by the fundamentalist Islamic clerics, want no modernization at all. They didn't even want telephones or telegraphs, and certainly not TV or radio (they carry Satan's messages). But the Saudi Royal Family either has slipped them in, or is slipping them in, at least for their own use (I'll bet their satellite dishes have more channels than ours do, Dammit!).

The clerics are furious about all this, but so what; they were probably against sliced bread and peanut butter, too. However, the Saudi Royal Family just may be going about this modernization, or at least the introduction of it, the wrong way. The perception among the public may be that only the elite have these modern, Satanic luxuries, and that sets the Saudi Royal Family apart from the average citizen even more. And that, as we know in modern times, breeds resentment. Lots of it. And if you think that resentment is strong before the masses get television, just wait until they do get it. And start hearing about how the world really is.

Say, how did a Royal Family ever work its way into Islam, anyway???

87. They don't execute enough literary critics.

One criticism is that they don't execute anal-retentive literary critics, those who don't appreciate a good satire when they come across one. But you know, other countries don't do that, either—it's just not a widespread practice. As repressive a regime as they run, they have never progressed to the point where they murder their literary critics, especially those who deal primarily with satirical works.

And maybe they have a point somewhere along the line. After all, an argument can be made that literary critics have a right to write what they want to, to disparage and criticize whatever they want to, without fear of any reprisals. It is a legitimate argument, at least in theory. But does it really work?

After all, if you don't execute them, they may keep right on doing exactly what they have been doing all along. And that would not be cool.

But maybe it is a matter for the United Nations, rather than for an individual country, to decide. And maybe after it has worked its way through all the proper channels of that great body, the troops can start moving and do what they need to do.

88. They have given money directly to persons who then gave it to terrorists.

Well, this one is more complicated than that, but there may be some truth in it. It was discovered that Princess Haifa al-Faisal, the wife of the Saudi ambassador to the U.S., Prince Bandar bin Sultan (The Old Wily Fox), had given regular payments of money, totaling thousands of dollars, to the family of a man who may have aided some of the 9/11 hijackers. Apparently, the money was supposed to have been used for medical payments for the man's wife, a Jordanian citizen, but Saudi critics seized upon the gifts to weigh in on the Saudis' seeming duplicitous attitude towards terrorism and its perpetrators. In the past, as we have noted earlier, some have accused the Saudis of "buying off" the terrorist elements, so that they would leave the Saudi Royal Family alone.

It will be interesting to see how these and other similar allegations shake out. The whole thing is probably symbolic of the uneasy relationship the Saudi Royal Family has with the people of Saudi Arabia (yet another example!). The Saudi Royal Family wants to stay in power and soak up the riches that have come its way over the years, and subjects tend to love their royal families (It's a clever concept, and one that has a solid psychological basis.). But at the same time, the Saudi people want bread, not just cake (Whew! Finally got that one out of the way!), and they are getting restless. Also, the Saudi people in general are more fundamentalist than the Saudi Royal Family (who need a break from all that stuff from time to time), so that explosive issue hangs in the immediate background.

89. Jerry Falwell said that Islam is a violent religion.

Or did he say that Mohammed was an advocate of violence, which is slightly different? Or something like that. And therefore, because the Saudi Royal Family is a very visible group of Islamists (is that a word?), they bear that heavy responsibility.

Now, Jerry Falwell has said a lot of things over the years, some of them very much in the mainstream, some of them seemingly silly. Many public figures fall into that category. Of course, it didn't help when, after Falwell made his statement about Islam being a violent religion, Muslims in India began a multi-day orgy of rioting and violence (yes, violence!). Talk about playing right into someone's hands! It's a little hard for critics of Falwell to pounce on him, when something he says comes true in the next day or so.

However violent Muslims may seem, we must remember that only an infinitesimal percentage of Muslims commit crimes, and even less commit violent crimes. And while terrorism is very bad, it kills many less individuals than war does. And we shouldn't forget that we have had, and continue to have, terrorism right in our own great country. Check into all of the bombings perpetrated in the past by white supremacists against people (mostly blacks, or in some cases, Jews), black churches, and synagogues.

90. Pat Robertson said that Muslims are "worse than the Nazis."

Oh, he did, did he? Well, yes, apparently he did.

He said that Muslims want to do worse things to the Jews than Nazis did. And in saying that, he stepped into one of the oldest traps to ever bedevil mankind: confusing the actions of some members of a group, however numerous, with the actions of all the members of the group. It has happened with every group in every direction (obviously, sometimes more in one direction than in the opposite direction), and it has struck certain individuals and groups that one would never have thunk would have been snared by that trap.

It is true that the most violent and intolerant members of a group are the ones who get the most attention, and many of the more moderate members sit back and say nothing in response, which seems to imply that they support the more radical view. However, that failure to repudiate the members who advocate violence and intolerance usually means more of a moral cowardice, a reluctance to get involved, than an acceptance of those radical viewpoints.

Let's face it: most Muslims are most concerned with where the next meal is coming from, how to put a roof over their heads, and so on—how to survive from day to day. With the sheer numbers of Muslims around the world, those are the ones that should be won over by any group, Jews or otherwise, who want to avoid long-term problems with Muslims in general.

Most Muslims, after all, are dirt poor. Which brings us back to that family in Saudi Arabia. You know—the one with no poor members.

91. Jimmy Swaggart called Mohammed a sex deviant.

As you can see, some of these reasons are somewhat indirect. This one, for example, would have you believe that Mohammed is a sex deviant, and therefore anyone who believes in him must be a pervert. Since the Saudi Royal Family is Islamic, and in the news almost daily, then . . .

Talk about the pot calling the kettle black on this one! Jimmy, is your memory that bad? Or have you straightened up, and want everyone else to as well? Of course, some involvement in sexual perversions (or is it preversions, Colonel Guano?) might keep some religious fanatics' hatred of life and mankind from flowering so violently—who knows?

As for the Saudi Royal Family, Jimmy Swaggart did not say to kill them, but who knows what one of his errant followers might do in a private moment. Those wild statements can fester in an unclean mind and erupt through the skin of humanity. Let's nip it in the bud.

As for sex deviance, it is common for individuals in very rich families to experiment here and there, so it would not be surprising if some members of the Saudi Royal Family fit Jimmy Swaggart's definition of a sex deviant. But they still shouldn't be killed for it . . .

92. Billy Graham Jr. called Islam an "evil and wicked religion".

Sometimes the Saudi Royal Family gets tarred with the overall negativism towards Islam, especially after 9/11. And there have been a lot of negative remarks about Islam in general, some of which we have dealt with elsewhere.

Billy Graham Jr., aka Franklin Graham, has indeed called Islam an "evil and wicked religion". And his sister, Anne Graham Lutz, who is also Billy Graham Sr.'s daughter, has also made what many would consider disparaging comments about Islam.

Of course, all this is very ironic in view of Billy Graham Sr. being caught red-handed on the 1972 Nixon tapes making disparaging comments about Jews and their influence on the politics of this country. Ordinarily, the televangelists try to cozy up to the Jewish community, or at least the portion of it that supports Israel the most. Of course, the reasons why televangelists support Israel are generally quite different from the reasons why American Jews support Israel, and it is likely that both groups know that very well, but continue in a sort of uncomfortable alliance for pure political reasons dealing with those limited issues.

But we seem to have strayed from the Saudi Royal Family, who most definitely should not be murdered because of anything that Billy Graham Jr. said.

93. They like President Bush a lot.

It is true that the Saudi Royal Family likes President Bush Jr. a lot, and they also liked President Bush Sr. a lot as well. That could be due to oil connections, but it is also partly due to long-term U.S. policy. Long-term U.S. policy is definitely linked to oil, but it is also partly a reward for the Saudis being one of the more moderate countries as far as Israel is concerned. They haven't attacked Israel directly, and we have recognized that.

Some political enemies of President Bush may wish the Saudi Royal Family harm just for political reasons, because they don't like him. After all, we must remember that some individuals weren't terribly unhappy (and may have even been happy) that President Reagan was shot and almost killed; they just wished the assassination attempt had worked. And of course, there were those who were not sorry that President Kennedy, or Bobby Kennedy, or Martin Luther King, were assassinated.

You can't stop people from feeling the way they do. The key is to keep them from acting on those feelings. And for that, we need for law enforcement to enforce the already existing laws against murder, if any such attempt is made on the lives of the Saudi Royal Family members. My God, if we all thought that way about political differences, we'd all be killing each other.

94. They liked President Clinton a lot.

Well, yes, they did. But so did a lot of other people. And you can expect that the Saudi Royal Family has probably liked every U.S. President since Saudi Arabia was formed. And you can bet that they will continue to like U.S. Presidents in the future, because I doubt that much will change in our relationship unless and until the Saudi Royal Family is overthrown, or pushed from office, or whatever. The linkage, both politically and economically, is too great.

But they did like President Clinton, as did a lot of foreign dignitaries. And we have to remember that Prince Bandar has been in Washington, DC since the 1980's, and he is a very charming fellow (He'll like it that I said that!).

President Clinton has a lot of political enemies, as does President Bush, as did President Reagan, and many of those political enemies have ice in their veins as far as how their particular political villains are dealt with. But that is no reason for the rest of us to become corrupted.

95. They use their friendships with U.S. government officials for special purposes.

This is what most sincere opponents of Saudi-U.S. relations would object to: a kind of favoritism such as no private citizen, and not many foreign governments, could enjoy.

During the investigation of the various individuals involved in the 9/11 terror attacks, it developed that the U.S. government had, on several occasions, refused to cooperate fully in providing other governments (Germany, for example) with important information that might link the terrorists with either high officials in the Saudi government, or with influential Saudi citizens. The FBI, in explaining its refusal, referred to legal agreements and diplomatic agreements that have been in effect for many years.

This is an excellent example of what people fear when they note Prince Bandar's friendship with many Presidents in a row, including President Bush Jr., and when they see him visiting the President at his Texas ranch along with other high Saudi officials. There is a general feeling among the public that we really have no stake in our government and its decisions, that it has been co-opted by wealthy foreigners for their secret purposes.

The people get frustrated when they see things like that. And masses of frustrated people sometimes act unpredictably on their frustration.

96. They aren't Muslim (or is it Moslem?) enough.

We've heard variations on this one before. They wear the gear and talk the talk in their own country, but once they leave and go to Western countries, they relax their standards.

Of course, like any blanket statement, this one is only partly true. After all, there are many members of the Saudi Royal Family, and it is unreasonable to expect that they all would be the same, or do things in the same way. Some do maintain the strict standards when they travel abroad, some do only to a lesser degree, and some swing way over to the more free-spirited side.

So the criticism has some validity, as many of them do tend to be more liberal in the company of Americans than they are inside Saudi Arabia. And one wonders how they can keep the dual lifestyle going forever. Already, they have many critics who realize what is going on, so it seems that it will be just a matter of time before the majority of their subjects know about it (the duality).

Like many political leaders, however, I suspect that they will bend with the prevailing wind, and in the long-term sense, that happens to be the gentle breeze of modernization. The key question is: will they survive the lengthy transition with their power intact? Modernization is like a multi-bladed knife that cuts against tradition at many points.

97. They always up oil production to save the U.S.'s bacon when there is a disruption of oil production.

It's kind of ironic that they would save anyone's bacon, now that I think about it. But it's true that they do. Of course, it gives them the opportunity to sell more oil, and to partially prevent other nations from stepping in more fully to fill the void. But it also shows, to some extent, the nature of the uneasy alliance between the Saudi Royal Family and high U.S. government officials (as distinguished from the "American people").

In truth, no country can raise the price of oil beyond a certain point for any great length of time, or it would have been done years ago. It's true that some of the Middle Eastern countries (at least the rulers) have made fortunes selling oil over the past three or more decades. But before that, Americans were making fortunes out in West Texas, and in Pennsylvania, doing the same thing. It's also true that, twice in the 1970's, Americans were caught unprepared for the cutbacks in oil supply, and the accompanying dramatic price rises. However, don't forget that major portions of those price increases corrected severely in the mid-1980's, to the extent that the economies of Texas, Louisiana, and Oklahoma were basically wrecked for many years.

Likewise, the economies of the Middle Eastern countries (and Mexico, and any country whose economy was greatly dependent on oil production and sales) were severely damaged, and have not really recovered to this day. Oil is pretty much all the Saudis have, and they have to use it wisely. It's still the cheapest fuel for many purposes, or it would have been replaced many years ago. Some day it will be replaced.

98. They have "ruined it" for Saudi businessmen to do business in the U.S.

Not long ago, a large hotel and convention center project in Kissimmee, Florida, backed by the very rich Alireza family, was canceled by Osceola County. The project was canceled because of protests from unions and local citizens opposed to the project because of the reported connections (however indirect) of both the Alireza family and the Saudi Royal Family to terrorist financing (Follow that money!!! Where is Deep Throat when we really need him?). The connection between the Alireza family and Osama bin Laden appeared somewhat indirect, but then that is how illicit funding works, whether in U.S. politics, or in worldwide terrorism.

However, there is no doubt that rumors can spread like wildfire, and cause very unfair consequences, and legitimate Saudi businessmen have cause to worry about some of the Saudi Royal Family's shenanigans. However, the flip side of that is that very few wealthy Saudis would ever have made their money without favoritism from the Saudi Royal Family in the first place. Apparently, nothing much gets done on a large commercial scale in Saudi Arabia without having a major "in" with the Saudi Royal Family. So any complaints from prominent Saudi businessmen (there are, of course, no prominent Saudi businesswomen, but if there were, you can bet they would have an even bigger "in" with the Saudi Royal Family!) are likely to fall on very unsympathetic ears in all four corners of the globe (except perhaps where it counts the most—in Washington, DC).

99. "All roads lead to Saudi Arabia" on funding of terrorism.

That's according to plaintiff's attorney Ronald L. Motley, of tobacco and asbestos litigation fame, who is representing the families of 9/11 victims in a lawsuit against 189 defendants, including six members of the Saudi Royal Family, as well as numerous banks, businesses, charities, and other individuals. Mr. Motley says that many influential Saudis, including members of the Saudi Royal Family, are up to their hairlines in the financing of terrorism. And what better motive could one have to just wipe out the whole family? What more reason could one possibly need?

Well now, hold on a moment there, Cowboy! Even Mr. Motley is fighting the alleged evildoers through the courts, with a lawsuit that could take many years. And the allegations are indeed just that at this point—allegations. They still have to be proven in court.

It is true, of course, that the Saudi government, along with its close allies in the U.S. government in Washington, DC, is actively trying its best to derail the lawsuit before it can even get to court. And that doesn't look good—no private citizen could do that. And the suit could be very embarrassing to the U.S. government, as it may very well uncover evidence that it has looked the other way, for geopolitical reasons, with regard to Saudi financing of terrorism, just as it has looked the other way regarding the Saudis' pure hatred of Israel.

We may just have to fall back on principle on this one . . .

100. They have issued a fatwa to kill the author of this work.

The fatwa, or religious ruling in Islam, was used against Salmon Rushdie after he published his novel, *The Satanic Verses*, back in 1989. Iranian clerics issued a ruling urging Muslims to track him down and assassinate him, and he is still in hiding today, even though the fatwa has supposedly been lifted. More recently, a fatwa was issued by Nigerian Muslims urging individual Muslims to kill the author of an article in a Nigerian newspaper that maintained that Muhammad would have married one of the Miss World contestants, had he lived in the present.

No such ruling has been issued related to the author of this work, at least as of the date of this writing.

101.They have failed to imprison large numbers of people who "don't get it."

I think we can end it on one that is definitely true. The Saudis, with all of their inclination for toughness on crime and sin, have utterly failed to incarcerate or otherwise discipline the extremely large numbers of people, both within Saudi Arabia and outside of it, who simply do not understand—specifically, those who don't get whether something is serious or comical, interesting or banal, controversial or of no interest whatsoever. They have failed, even though the evidence is overwhelming, as clear as ever a case of adultery was ever proved in the Desert Kingdom.

The fundamentalists may have the Saudi Royal Family looking over its collective shoulder on this one, as they would definitely know what to do.

Printed in the United States
110813LV00002B/51/A

9 781413 405293